California Politics

Study Tools

R. L. COHEN

Humanities

ACADEMIC PUBLISHERS

Humanities
ACADEMIC PUBLISHERS

ISBN: 9781988557885

Published in New Zealand and the United States of America

Humanities Academic Publishers

A catalogue record for this book is available from the National Library of New Zealand.

Kei te pātengi raraunga o Te Puna Mātauranga o Aotearoa te whakarārangi o tēnei pukapuka.

CONTENTS

CHAPTER 1

EARLY CALIFORNIA

Expeditions in California

- **The contacts of Europeans** with California started in the mid-1530s when the men of Hernan Cortez entered Baja California.

- In 1542, the Spaniards sailed north to Alta California, and the expedition of Juan Rodriguez Cabrillo's expedition was the first to made landings as far north as modern Santa Barbara.

- In this regard, the Spanish navigator Juan Rodriguez Cabrillo was *the first European* to discover California in 1542.

- During this period, the territory was inhabited by about *130,000 Native Americans*.

- The territory did not receive proper attention from Spain for more than two centuries because of the **enormous poverty** in the region as well as the general slowdown of the Spanish exploration.

California's Missions and Growth

- The foundation of Spanish missions in California had an enormous historical significance for the west part of the country but also for the whole state.

- The **economic success** of these missions proves the development of the economically viable community in circumstances of extremely limited resources.

- The case of Spanish California is unique when trying to portray the Spanish conquest's effects in terms of **economic growth and prosperity**.

- In a short period, California managed to transfer from a struggling frontier bastion to economically independent by 1810 and *independent* from the Spanish empire by 1821.

- While domestic events did not influence political independence, economic independence resulted from the *development* of the missions.

- During the Mission's period, each mission became an economic community built by the labor of the local Native Californians.

- The earliest studies of the Spanish California missions present the bad treatment of the local Native people. In this regard, the **death rate**, especially among women and children, was high.

- The labor of the Native people was compensated for *food, clothes, and beads.*

- By joining the missions, the Natives needed to build churches, housing, warehousing, and manufacturing facilities.

Mission Basilica San Diego de Alcala

- The Spanish have been the founders of 21 Mission along the coast of California in the late 18th century. The Mission of San Diego de Alcalá represents a very significant part of the nation's Spanish heritage because it was the first mission formed by the Spanish.

- It was founded by Father Serra in 1769, together with the first Spanish colony and the presidio in Alta California.

- The first Spanish colony – San Diego, was formed on July 1, 1769.

Old Mission San Luis Rey de Francia

- The Mission of San Luis was established in 1798 by Father Lasuen, the successor of Father Serra.

- The Mission of San Luis was the only Mission to be named after a king, St. Louis of France.

- Shortly after Mexico won its independence, the law on secularization passed.

- From 1847-1857 the Mission was used as an operational base by U.S. soldiers.

Mission of San Juan Capistrano

- The mission of San Juan Capistrano was founded on November 1, 1776, and it was the 7th mission formed. This mission is the beginning of what would later be called Orange County.

- The mission was destroyed just one month after the founding by the Kumeyaay military formation.

Mission of San Gabriel Archangel

- The mission of San Gabriel Archangel was founded on September 8, 1771, and it is the 4th mission by order of creation.

- Founded on the hills north of modern-day Montebello but moved to its current location in 1775.

- The San Gabriel Mission was one of the most prosperous missions since it has owned a quarter of the livestock and grain of all missions.

- The mission's most prosperous period was in 1829, when the mission's herds consisted of 25,000 cattle and 15,000 sheep.

- The mission architecture is very reminiscent of the Moorish fortress, similar to the style of the cathedral in Cordoba

- Its founders were Fathers Serra, Pedro Benito Cambón, and Angel Fernandez Somera y Balbuena.

- It was at this mission that Fr. José Zalvidea introduced the first of California's large-scale vineyards.

- The Viceroy and inspector general had the privilege to choose the name of San Gabriel Archangel, which gave the right of choosing the fathers of the new mission to father Junipero.

The Mission of San Fernando Rey de Espana

- The Mission of San Fernando Rey de Espana was founded on September 8, 1797, by the Franciscans.

- The exact place of the mission was in the north part of the Valley, which the Native Americans called Achois Comihabit.

- In the first year, the mission operated in a building in ownership of Francisco Reyes, Alcalde of the Pueblo of Los Angeles, in the period until the first church was being constructed.

- The church was built in 1798, along with the Priests' dwelling. The permanent church was completed in 1806.

- By this time, there were about 1,000 Native people at the Mission; their village had 70 houses and its plaza.

Old Mission of San Buenaventura

- The old Mission of San Buenaventura was founded on Easter Sunday on March 30, 1749, and it was the last mission founded by the priest Junipero Serra.

- The most important feature of this church is that it was close to the water, a fact that meant a lot at that time. Thus, the living conditions in this mission were much more manageable in terms of garden maintenance, plant irrigation, food mirroring, etcetera.

- Unfortunately, the entire irrigation system that was built was destroyed in 1862 by floods that swept through the region.

California during Mexico Independence

- At the beginning of the 19th century, the Spanish colonies in America struggled for their **independence**.

- California felt the effects of these movements in terms of limited supplies to the missions, the pressure of the navy making them *unable to spare ships and to bring supplies and other needed products* for the missions and villages north of San Diego.

- The main trading partners in this period were *England, Russia, France, and the USA.*

- Mexico achieved independence in 1821.

- The most important change brought by the Mexican independence was the secularization of the missions and limiting the control of the Franciscan missionaries. This kind of process of **secularization** started in 1834.

- In the beginning, the Franciscans administered the lands of missions for the Natives that lived here when the **missioners** arrived, but only some of them benefited at the end of the mission system.

- Like the mission system, Native Californians provided the biggest part of the working force for the emerging ranching economy. Some of the Spanish-speaking Natives married working-class Mexicans and further complicated the already complicated racial categories.

- During the 1830s and 1840s, increasing numbers of Europeans and Americans arrived in California *wishing to start a life in the land of California.*

- Although the successful start of its **independence**, Mexico was faced with difficulties in ruling the Californian province.

- The last governor who was sent to California from Mexico was Manuel Micheltorena, who came to California in 1842.

- Much of California was unrecognizable to Native groups that had witnessed the coming of the Spaniards less than 80 years before, by the time the US-Mexican War broke out in 1846.

Mexican – American war

- The Mexican-American war (1846-1848) was the first conflict that the **USA fought on foreign ground.**

- The American president James K. Polk believed that the USA had a *manifest destiny* to expand the American influence through the whole continent reaching the Pacific and confronted the politically divided and militarily weak Mexico.

- The Mexican – American war started on April 25, 1846, with the attack of the Mexican cavalry on a group of American soldiers in the disputed zone under the command of General Zachary Taylor.

- These battles were the reason for Congress to **declare war** on May 13.

- It is interesting that *no declaration of War ever came from Mexico.*

- During the conflict between the soldiers, many diseases and illnesses prevailed.

- Infection and disease claimed many more lives in the United States than in the war. At least 10,000 soldiers died of disease, while about 1,500 were killed in action or wounded in battle (estimates of **war casualties** vary).

CHAPTER 2

THE RISE OF
THE SOUTHERN PACIFIC

Introduction

- In its most prosperous days, the *Southern Pacific* was the most influential company in California.

- Founded in 1865, the railway connected two main cities - **San Francisco and San Diego**. In 1868 extended its routes to New Orleans.

- I 1885, its routes spread over the Central Pacific Railroad, which was the western half of the nation's *first transcontinental railroad*.

- With the help of Southern Pacific, **Pacific Electric** has become one of the largest intercity electric rail networks.

- Southern Pacific also had a considerable passenger train lane in California, most notably the Daytime Running Lights between Los Angeles and San Francisco.

- The construction of the Southern Pacific Railroad marks a turning point in US history and a moment of **national unification**.

- It was a realization of *Manifest destiny*. The six-month trip to California from other parts of the continent was reduced to two weeks.

- In just a few years, this line helped to develop the western parts of the continent through European-American settlement, business, and trade development, and the end of indigenous life in these parts of the continent.

The importance of the Southern Pacific railroad

- The Southern Pacific railroad brought the West part of the country to the world and the world to the West because it helped California to move *from a once-isolated place to a significant economic and political force* and helped lead to the **state's rapid growth**.

- It also made travel more affordable. If travel across the USA was accounted for $20,000 (in today's dollars), the use of the railroads allowed cheaper traveling.

- Furthermore, it helped to develop postal traffic. In 1872, the first mail-order catalog was started by Aaron Montgomery Ward.

- The impacts of the construction of the railways were also **negative**.

- During the construction of the railway, a large part of the forests was destroyed, the wilderness was no longer inaccessible.

- The railroad establishments made it possible for hunters to travel westward and kill millions of buffalo.

- **Racial conflicts** increased.

The Big Four

- Theodore Judah, a civil engineer who designed California's first railroad, promoted **Route 41**, passing through Nebraska, Wyoming, Utah, Nevada, and California.

- His opponents noted the considerable obstacles to his proposal, the most serious of which was the *Sierra Nevada mountain range*.

- The first people to agree to give the needed support to Judah's idea were Collis P. Huntington and his partner, Mark Hopkins; dry goods merchant Charles Crocker; and wholesale grocer, soon to be governor, Leland Stanford.

  – These backers would later become known as the **"Big Four"**.

- Huntington and his partners paid Judah to do the necessary research.

- During the presentation of the idea to Congress in October 1861, Judah used maps from his **research**.

- Many members of Congress opposed the idea of *building a railroad because of the high cost*, especially during the Civil War.

- However, President Abraham Lincoln, an avid supporter of the railroad, **agreed**.

- On July 1, 1862, Lincoln signed the Pacific Railroad Act, approving $ 32,000 inland and government bonds per mile of the railroad to two companies, the *Central Pacific Railway* and *the Pacific Rail Union*.

- Immediately after this act, conflicts arose between Judah and his business partners. In October 1863, Judah traveled to New York City in search of investors to cover his Sacramento partners. He did not survive the trip.

- The Big Four replaced Judah with **Samuel Montego,** and construction teams in the Central Pacific began building the line east of Sacramento.

- Over three years, 80 % of the Central Pacific workforce was made up of Chinese workers, as they proved to be a critical factor in advancing the line across the Sierra Nevada.

- The Chinese workers accomplished amazing and dangerous feats no other workers would or could do.

CHAPTER 3

THE RISE OF CALIFORNIA'S PROGRESSIVISM

Introduction

- The importance of the **California railway** was excellent in terms of the development of the overall social, economic and political life.

- According to some historians, the railroad has *increased California's growth and development,* while others see a source of *corruption and scandal.*

- In 1910, the Progressives *took control of the Republican Party* in the country.

- They nominated **Hiram Johnson**, an avid lawyer, and anti-railroad advocate, to run for Governor. In this regard, Johnson's credit is immense.

Hiram Johnson

- He was the leader of the Progressive party in California and reform governor of California in the period between 1911 – 1917.

- In 1910 Johnson being a member of the *Lincoln – Roosevelt league,* won the elections for Governor (National Governors Association).

- This League was famous because of its characteristics as a Progressive Republican movement opposed to the **Southern Pacific Railroad.**

- He was the leader of the Progressive party in California and reform governor of California in the period between 1911 – 1917.

- In 1910 Johnson being a member of the *Lincoln – Roosevelt league*, won the elections for Governor (National Governors Association).

- This League was famous because of its characteristics as a Progressive Republican movement opposed to the **Southern Pacific Railroad**.

- He was known for his unwavering **isolationism**, opposing U.S. support for the Treaty of Versailles, the League of Nations, and the *Permanent Court of International Justice* known as the World Court.

- He was a major sponsor of acts of **neutrality** in the 1930s, opposed to preparations for World War II and the formation of the United Nations.

The rise of nonpartisan candidates during progressivism

- Johnson's election as Governor of California in 1910 marked a **turning point** in California's overall political history.

- Most of the changes introduced then are *still in force today*.

- Progressives believed that both political parties were *influenced by the Southern Pacific Monopoly*.

- In **nonpartisan elections**, no label of a political party may appear next to the candidate's name, nor is financial party support permitted for candidates.

- This system consisted of high criteria that candidates had to meet to qualify for the job. Previously, *political parties have traditionally rewarded their activists*, party members with local government jobs, a process known as patronage.

- Hiring professional managers to run operations is also a credit to **progressives**.

- Reforms in California during the Progressives provided greater **transparency and accountability** for both institutions and elected officials.

- To enable the disclosure of all matters of the public institutions and the fact that the elected representatives *will first serve the people and will not put the personal interest before the general one*, different laws have been adopted.

- Such laws are often referred to as "**sunshine laws**" because they are based on the principles of transparency and accountability.

Merit system

- The **merit system** evolved gradually. Although the merit system prevails today, *political patronage* still exists at all levels of government, but with a much lower degree of representation than before.

- On June 16, 1913, the **California State Legislature** approved the State Civil Service Bill (Chapter 590 of Statutes 1913), and Republican Governor Hiram Johnson signed it.

- This bill established the **California State Civil Service Commission** to oversee California's newly established civil service system.

Proposition 13

- The most important part of the act is its first paragraph, which determines **the tax rate for real estate**. According to this paragraph, the maximum amount of any ad valorem tax on real property *shall not exceed one percent of the total cash value of such property.*

- Proposition 13 reduces the property taxes by accessing values at their 1976 value and restricted annual increases of assessed value to an inflation factor not to exceed 2% per year.

- Proposition 13 prohibits **reassessment** of a new base year value *except in change of ownership and completion of new construction.*

- The other important part of the initiative is that requires a **two-thirds majority** in both legislative houses for future increase of any state tax rates or amounts of revenue collected including *income tax rates.*

- It also requires a two-thirds vote majority in local elections for local governments which aim to increase **special taxes**.

- One year after Proposition 13 passed, property tax revenue dropped by 60%.

CHAPTER 4

HYPER DIVERSITY
OF THE POPULATION

Introduction

- From 1960 to 1970, the working-age population grew by a little more than 6 million—a slow expansion driven by the relatively small birth cohorts in the late 1930s and early 1940s.

- The figure of **6 million additional working-age** people reflects the balance of a net increase of almost 9 million in the third-plus generation population and a net decrease of almost 2.5 million in first and second-generation populations.

- These figures reflect *the mortality experience and aging out of the workforce* (attaining age 65) of immigrants and children from early in the 20th century, before the long immigration pause.

- According to experts, **migration** is described as a two-way process under the influence of push factors from Mexico and pulls factors from the United States.

- **Western Mexico**, and especially the states of Michoacán, Jalisco, and Guanajuato, is a source of immigrants to the United States. Since the MMP survey, migration rates have increased from 3.7 to 7.5 percent during the analyzed period.

- The continuous increase in migration is related to the 1970s and 1980s, *increasing almost 10% in 1988.*

The Bracero Program

- The main cause of mass immigration from Mexico was the **Bracero program**, implemented since 1942.

- This program allowed temporary legal migration from Mexico to the United States to *make up for labor shortages* in the United States due to the war.

- At the time this program was active, more than 200,000 immigrants entered the United States each year.

- Most of them were concentrated in California, Arkansas, Texas, Arizona, and New Mexico.

- The unexpected end of the program increased the rate of **illegal immigration**.

Factors of Illegal Immigration

- One of the main drivers of illegal migration is **higher wages and more jobs** in the United States.

- Another factor is the failure to *implement laws that would prevent illegal immigration*, such as IRCA employer sanctions, signal tolerance for illegal immigration.

- *Family contacts and networks* are the ones that provide direct information to immigrants. The Bracero Program is undoubtedly responsible for this.

Mexico, Latin, and Central American migration

- As a labor force, Mexicans were transformed into the California economy, working predominantly in the **manufacturing sector**.

- What is characteristic of early Mexican mass immigration is the fact that black workers were considered to be most affected by the **influx of lower-income immigrants**.

- However, over time, black workers began to see an *available upgrade* in their professional status.

- Most of the United States has been hit by large waves of immigration, including California.

- In the 1980s, a **quarter** of all legal immigrants to the United States lived in California.

- Concerns about Mexican immigration stem not only from a large number of immigrants but also from a large number of illegal immigrants with low levels of education and qualifications, as well as **poor knowledge of English**.

- Of Mexican immigrants, two-thirds of those living in Los Angeles have settled since 1970, and more than half arrived in the second half of the decade.

- Of the non-Hispanic group, most arrived before the 1970s, mostly from Europe and after 1970 from Asia. As mentioned above, the most significant cause for concern is **illegal immigration**.

- After the manufacturing sector, the following areas where Mexican immigrants work are the **service sector, sales, and commerce**, where one in 6 and one in 7 employees are Mexican immigrants.

Gentrification

- **Gentrification** is a process of changes in the neighborhood that implicates economic changes in what used to be a historically not so developed area, in terms of real estate investment and *new higher-income residents moving in*.

- Newcomers often have **different views** on many issues from the natives, such as environment, community understanding, economic development.

- In many gentrification communities across the United States, domestic migration accompanied by all the economic, political, cultural, and social influences increases the sense of **class differentiation**.

- The processes of gentrification undoubtedly influenced the change of **real estate markets**.

- Home prices in Missoula more than tripled during the 1990s.

- The influence of gentrification can be *both negative and positive*.

- Communities react differently to gentrification so to craft effective **policies**.

- **Policymakers** need to understand how different kinds of communities experience the process.

Latino immigrants in Rural America

- During the last decades, Rural America has become an attractive place for richer Americans that want to build a **paradise house far from the messy city.**

- Latinos are *mainly concentrated in larger cities.*

- In analyzing the rural dimensions of Latino settlements, geographers and other scholars take into account the following interrelated issues: the changing nature of *labor markets in rural areas* and the *withdrawal of immigrants to non-traditional destinations.*

CHAPTER 5

RECALLS IN CALIFORNIA

Introduction

- According to article 2 from the Californian Constitution, the citizens of this state have the right to **initiate a recall election**.

- This rule applies both to state and local officials but does not apply to federal officials.

- Also, citizens can recall *judges* of courts of appeal and trial courts.

Procedure

1. The proponent fills a **notice of intent** to recall petition that needs to be signed by 65 voters to start the petition drive process.

2. In the actual petition, **signatures** must be equal to the percentage of the total number of votes most recently cast for the targeted office, i.e., 12% for executive officials and 20% for state legislators and judges.

3. The petition must consist of signatures of each of at least five counties *equal in number to 1% of the last vote for the office in that county.*

State officials

- For the officials of a city, county, school district, county board of education, or any resident voting district, **signatures** from the following percentage of registered voters is required:

- 30% in jurisdictions with 0 - 1,000 registered voters;
- 25% in jurisdictions with 1,000 - 10,000 registered voters;
- 20% in jurisdictions with 10,000 - 50,000 registered voters;
- 15% in jurisdictions with 50,000 - 100,000 registered voters;
- 10% in jurisdictions with 100,000 or more registered voters

County judges

- According to section 14 of Article 2 of the California Constitution, the required petition for a recall is **20% of the votes cast for the judge** in the last election, rather than a percentage registered.
- In the case of a county superior court judge position that did not appear on the ballot at the last relevant election, signatures equaling 20% of votes cast for whichever countywide office received *the least total number of votes in the most recent general election* in the judge's county must be collected to qualify a recall of the judge for the **ballot**.

Language

- The language in the recall provision is strictly procedural. Substantive grounds for recalls are not specified.
- Recalls can be launched to remove corrupt officials and to remove officials whose policies and performance are found wanting.

Basic concepts

- Notice of intent
- Delivery to the officer to be recalled
- Publication of the notice of intent
- Official's answer
- Sample ballot
- Petition form
- Replacement candidates
- State recall

- Local recall
- Election results
- On the election ballot, voters are asked the following:
    - Shall [name of officer sought to be recalled] be recalled (removed) from the office of [title of office]? Additionally, under the recall question, the ballot will include a list of candidates to take the place of official submitted for recall in the event of a successful recall vote. The list of candidates must include a space for voters to write in a candidate of their own.

Controversies

- Recalls are associated with:
- Populism
- Politization of corruption
- Distrust of the masses

Open primary elections

- The most significant developments in the laws regulating elections can be found in the legislation in the various states from 1913.
- These provisions mainly focus on strengthening the direct primary for party nominations, the growth of the non-partisan primary and election for judges and municipal officers, the gradual adoption of the short ballot principle, and the extension of "**corrupt practices prevention**" measures.
- Under new California laws, **voters receive by mail sample primary ballots** (if they are registered for the primaries) and sample election ballots.
- A new check against fraudulent ballots is the use in Nevada of specially water-marked paper, arranged to show the watermark when the ballot is folded, the design to be changed from year to year.

Proposition 62

- Proposition 62 refers to a single primary ballot in which all state and congressional candidates are presented together, no matter their **party affiliation**.
- The top two candidates with the most votes for each office should appear on the general election ballot, even if one of the two received a *majority of the vote* (80-90% of the votes), even if both were of the same party.

CHAPTER 6

DIRECT DEMOCRACY: CALIFORNIA INITIATIVE'S PROCESS

Introduction

- How **direct democracy** is enacted in California?

- As specified by Article II of the California Constitution, citizens can initiate legislation in several ways, either as a constitutional amendment or a state statute.

- Ballots are usually held to resolve the most controversial issues – tax measures have been the most recurrent ones - and they thus generate passionate debates across the State.

The initiative process

- **Direct initiatives** are those where voters place a proposed statute or an amendment to the constitution directly on the ballot.

- Instead, **indirect initiatives** are those where proponents collect signatures and then present the measure to the legislature for enactment.

Direct initiatives

- The procedure to qualify a proposal for the ballot must follow a specific procedure. The first step is **writing the proposed law** by the proponents of the initiative.

- Having written the proposal, proponents submit the text - together with their contact information and a signed statement to certify that they are qualified electors - to the 'California Attorney General's Initiative Coordinator,' with a request to prepare a title and one hundred words summary for the circulation.

- Proponents must also disclose in a separate document who are the top official funders of the initiative and *deposit 2000$*, a sum that will be refunded in case the initiative goes to the ballot within the following two years.

- **Collectors** can be paid according to the number of signatures collected, but those breaching the elections code with abuses - such as false statements about the content or effect of the petition or giving money in exchange for the signature - can incur *criminal penalties*.

- The number of signatures required to place a measure on the ballot varies according to the **initiative**.

- If valid signatures are less than 95%, the initiative failed. If valid signatures are between 95-110% of the amount required, then each signature must be **"fully checked."**

- Finally, if valid signatures are greater than 110%, the proposition qualifies for the ballot *without further certification*.

- Due to the problems that may occur in this phase, proponents usually seek *at least 50 percent more than the legal minimum* number of signatures to compensate for possible invalid signatures.

Indirect initiatives

- In 1911, the **California legislature** had the power to get involved if the initiative's proponents so desired.

- The process itself promoted this measure since proponents had to gather signatures of *only at least 5% of the total votes cast at the last gubernatorial election* with the legislature's involvement. In comparison, this number increased to 8% for direct initiatives.

- Nowadays, 10 out of the 24 American states that allow for the initiative include *indirect initiatives*.

California recall process

- Citizens in California can remove their **state and local officials** before their term expires, but they cannot remove *federal officers*, who are instead subject to the US constitution.

- Whereas federal offices were more independent, because they had to represent the whole country rather than a specific state, local representatives were considered servants of the people of that state, who then had the right to direct politicians in every decision.

- Once Governor receives all documents, a notice for the recall election is published not less than 60 days nor more than 80 days from the date of certification of sufficient signatures.

- The election must take place **within 180 days** from the same date.

- The procedure for the recall of '**Local Officers**' is similar to the one for '**State Officers**' since the delivery, publication, drafting, and circulation phase are the same.

- Instead, the number of signatures required and the deadlines for the submission of the signatures change since they both differ according to the number of registered voters in the electoral jurisdiction.

- In this case, elections must take place *between 88 and 125 days after the date of certification* that sufficient signatures have been collected.

- In sum, the recall process is meant to address two main issues.

- On the one side, the removal of officials who are no longer acting in the public interest because they have become corrupted by **corporate interests**.

- On the other side, the punishment of an official **who is not acting as promised during the elections**. There are divided opinions on the efficiency of these measures and on which features ought to be *improved*.

California recall process and money

- The importance of money investment in initiative procedures can be well noted by considering the list of the most expensive ballots in California, of which **all ten most expensive occurred over the last two decades**.

- The most expensive Proposition in California history was *Proposition 22* in 2020, which was an initiated statute to define *app-based drivers* as independent contractors rather than employees or agents.

Reform proposals

- Suggestions **to improve the initiative process are divided** between those who argue in favor of increasing the legislature's role and those who sustain instead that more popular deliberation is required.

- It may seem that solutions must require an increase in the legislature's involvement or the judiciary. Nevertheless, some have also argued to render the initiative process more deliberative.

- Citizens' direct participation is essential in any democracy, since not only it balances the will of the majority with the need to protect minority interest, but it also favors mechanisms for *fact-finding, debate, consensus building, and for understanding better what laws imply.*

Direct democracy and public policy

- Direct democracy is connected to various improvements concerning the citizens' **political participation**.

- For example, younger citizens and those more interested in the political process are more supportive of direct democracy.

- Direct democracy has several **economic implications**.

- For example, states employing initiative procedures seem to lead to better economic performances.

- Acknowledging the **hybrid nature** of California's democracy does not entail that direct initiatives are just tools in the hands of a few political elites.

- Research demonstrates that direct democracy is powerful in shaping directly and indirectly public policy in the States where it is used and that direct democracy produces positive outcomes *both from the instrumental and the educative point of view.*

CHAPTER 7

THE EXECUTIVE BRANCH

Introduction

- The Governor of a state or province is the executive head of government in any democratic country and serves as a *link between the state and federal governments*.
- **The Governor of California** is the head of the State's executive branch.
- They are chosen for a four-year term and may be re-elected by California for a second term.

California Constitution

- California's current Constitution was adopted in 1879 and has been revised *516 times* as of 2020.
- The executive branch of the State of California is dealt with under Article V of the Constitution.
- There are 13 sections in Article V, numbered 1 through 14, with no section 12.
- The Governor has the **supreme executive power in the State**, according to Section 1 of the Constitution.

Laws

- California's laws are administered and enforced by the executive branch.
- The California executive branch is made up of over **200 state institutions** and is led by the Governor.
- The people of California elect the branch's executive authorities, such as *the Governor, Lieutenant Governor, Secretary of State, and Attorney General,* and others.

Key actors

- The Governor, Lieutenant Governor, Secretary of State, Attorney General, State Controller, State Treasurer, Insurance Commissioner, and State Superintendent of Public Instruction **are the eight constitutional officers who serve statewide.**

- The **Governor of California** is the most influential figure in the State's executive branch. He is elected by the people of California and is limited to two four-year Terms. Some of his roles and duties:

- The **State Address** is delivered to members of the Legislature at the start of each legislative session. The annual budget is presented to the Legislature, together with projected revenue and cost statements. The ability to veto any bill enacted by the Legislature and return it to the house of origin with his concerns.

- **Appropriation legislation** is subject to *line-item veto power*.

- For consideration and approval by the **Legislature**, Governor prepares and submits annual or biennial budget proposals to the Legislature for *consideration and approval*.

- Governors in several states, commonwealths, and territories have the authority to exercise "reduction" veto power (also known as "line-item" or "line-item" veto power), which allows them to remove appropriations from budgets that they oppose.

- The **California State Guard** is an integral part of the State's integrated disaster and emergency response system in today's world.

- The **National Guard** provides a trained military force with unique capabilities. It collaborates seamlessly with our National Guard counterparts, federal agencies, State and local governments, and non-governmental relief organizations *to provide critical assistance when required.*

- In the event of a vacancy, the **Lieutenant Governor** becomes Governor, according to the Constitution.

- In the Governor's *absence from the State, temporary infirmity, or impeachment*, the Lieutenant Governor will function as acting Governor. The Lieutenant Governor is also President of the Senate, although solely with a casting vote.

- A **casting vote** is used to break a tie in a vote. Only the casting vote may be utilized if it will produce the requisite majority.

- The **Secretary of State** is California's chief elections officer, in charge of overseeing and certifying elections and inspecting and certifying voting technology for use in the State.

- The Secretary of State **maintains a detailed record of all official acts of the state legislature and executive departments**. The Secretary is in charge of the enrolled copy of the Constitution, all acts and resolutions approved by the Legislature, each house's Journals, the Great Seal of California, and all books, documents, deeds, parchments, maps, and papers retained or deposited in the office subject to the law.

- The **Attorney General** is responsible *for implementing California's laws consistently and fairly and assisting district attorneys,* local law enforcement, and federal and international criminal justice agencies in administering justice.

- The Attorney General's constitutional responsibilities are carried out through the *Department of Justice's programs.*

- The Department's legal programs represent the people in civil and criminal cases before California and federal trial, appellate, and supreme courts.

- The State **Treasurer** is the government's banker, investor, and asset manager.

- The Treasurer invests money on behalf of the State, cities, counties, schools, and other local governments. The Treasurer is in charge of selling and administering the *State's bond program, which includes voter-approved infrastructure bonds.*

- The Treasurer is a member of the California Public Employees' Retirement System (CalPERS), the State Teachers' Retirement System (CalSTRS), and the California Housing Finance Agency's boards of directors (CalHFA).

- The **State Controller** is the State's chief financial officer. The State Controller's primary responsibilities include:

  1. providing sound fiscal control over both public fund receipts and disbursements;

  2. reporting on the financial operations and condition of both state and local governments regularly;

  3. ensuring that money owed to the State is collected through fair, equitable, and effective tax administration;

  4. providing financial guidance to local governments

CHAPTER 8

CALIFORNIA COURT SYSTEM

Introduction

- The judiciary in the United States has a **dual court system**, with courts at both the national and state levels.

- Both levels have three basic tiers consisting of *trial courts*, *appellate courts*, and finally *courts of last resort*, typically called supreme courts, at the top.

- However, as a state itself creates each state's court system, each one differs in structure, the number of courts, and even name and jurisdiction.

- The state court system in California has two types of state courts:

  1. trial courts (also called "superior courts");
  2. and appellate courts.

Trial courts

- **Trial courts** are also known as "superior courts." In the trial or superior court, a judge, and sometimes a jury, hears testimony and evidence and decides a case by applying the law to the facts of the case.

- In the whole state of California, there are *58 superior courts, 1 in each county*.

- Trial court judges are elected at a general election by voters of the county on a nonpartisan ballot.

Appeal courts

- When a defendant loses a case or part of a case in the trial court, one can appeal this decision in a higher court (an appellate court) to review the trial court's decision.

- Appeals of family law cases, probate cases, juvenile cases, felony cases, and civil cases for more than $25000 are heard in Courts of Appeal.

- In each **Court of Appeal**, a panel of 3 judges (justices) decides appeals from trial courts.

- Each district (or division) has a *presiding justice and two or more associate justices.*

- The **Courts of Appeal** have to provide a mandatory review of jurisdiction.

- There are 6 Courts of Appeal, and each of them covers a specific number of counties in California.

- The district headquarters for Courts of Appeal is located in *San Francisco, Los Angeles, San Diego, Fresno, and San Jose.*

California Supreme Court

- The Supreme Court is the **state's highest court**.

- It can *review cases* decided by the Courts of Appeal.

- Also, certain kinds of cases go directly to the Supreme Court.

- They are not heard first in a Court of Appeal, such as death penalty appeals and disciplinary cases involving judges

- There are **seven justices** on the Supreme Court, and at least four must agree to decide.

- The 7 includes 1 Chief Justice and six associate justices, appointed by the Governor, confirmed by the Commission on Judicial Appointments, and by the public at the next general election.

Federal courts

- In parallel to state courts, in each state function, federal courts that deal with cases that refer to the U.S. government, the U.S. Constitution, or federal laws.

- However, federal courts usually *do not deal with cases related to* divorce and child custody, probate and inheritance, real estate, juvenile matters, criminal charges, contract disputes, traffic violations, or personal injury.

- **Bankruptcy** cases are only handled by federal courts.

Collaborative couts

- **Collaborative courts**, also known as *problem-solving courts*, combine judicial supervision with rehabilitation services that are monitored and focused on recovery to reduce recidivism and improve offender outcomes.

  1. They integrate services with justice system processing.

  2. They aim to achieve the desired goals without using the traditional adversarial process.

  3. Early and prompt identification of eligible participants for the program.

  4. They provide access to a variety of services, such as treatment and rehabilitation services.

Diversity in the court system

- According to demographic statistics of the **judicial branch of California** (2020), 37.4% of all judges in the state were women, and 62.6% were men.

- However, the ratio between male and female judges was significantly lower in the Supreme Court (42.9% to 57.1%) than in Trial Courts (37.4% to 62.6%).

- It is important to mention that the total number of female judges increased from 28.3% in 2008 to 37.4% in 2020.

- In terms of **racial variations**, differences are depending on the court level.

- In the **Trial Courts**, 65.2% of all judges were declared to be White, 11.2% had Hispanic or Latino origins, and respectively 7.9% and 7.6% were Asian or Black/African American. In the Court of Appeal, the ratio of judges reported as *White grew to 73.5%.*

- On the level of the **Supreme Court**, White and Asian judges (two judges each) represent 28.6% each. Three other judges declared to be either Black/African American, Hispanic/Latino, or Some Other Race. Over time the total ratio of judges that declared to be *White decreased from 72.5% in 2008 to 65.6% in 2020.*

- In terms of variation regarding gender identity/sexual orientation, respondents declared to be Heterosexual at each level.

- The *least* at the Trial Court level (71.3%) and the *most* at the Supreme Court level (100%).

- In terms of the other respondents, at the Trial Court level, 1.5% declared to be Lesbian, 2% to be Gay, and 0.1% to be either Bisexual or Transgender. 25.1% did not provide an answer.

- At the Court Appeal level, 2% declared to be Lesbian (2 respondents), 1% to be Gay (1 respondent). 18.6% of respondents did not provide an answer.

Fundamental concepts

1. Pretrial, trial, and post-trial.
2. Infraction.
3. Misdemeanor.
4. Felony.
5. Arraignment.
6. Preliminary hearing.
7. Both criminal and civil cases can be appealed.

Administration of Californian courts

- The **Judicial Council** is the governing body of the California courts. The **California Supreme Court** Chief Justice chairs it.

- The **California Constitution** directs the Judicial Council to provide policy guidelines to the courts, make recommendations annually to the Governor and Legislature, and adopt and revise California Rules of Court in the areas of court administration, practice, and procedure.

- The council has 21 voting members, including 14 judges appointed by the Chief Justice,

- four attorneys appointed by the State Bar Board of Trustees,

- one member from each house of the Legislature,

- and two non-voting members who are court administrator.

Criminal Justice and Prison System in California

- The prison system in California includes various types of facilities like *prisons, fire camps, contract beds, reentry programs,* and other programs administered by the state-owned agency - **California Department of Corrections and Rehabilitation** (CDCR), with its headquarters in Sacramento.

- CDCR owns and operates 34 prisons throughout the state and operates one prison leased from a private company.

- Types of facilities in California:

    1. City and Country Jails.
    2. State prisons.
    3. Federal prisons.
    4. ICE detention centers.
    5. Juvenile facilities.
    6. Camps.

- As maintenance of prison facilities and the cost of incarceration are expensive, states have an incentive to cut prison costs, and one of the means to do it is **privatization.**

- Suppose a state hinges its willingness to contract with a private corporation upon the corporation's ability to offer *a bid 5 to 10% lower than current state expenditures.*

California Innocence Project

- California Western School of Law (San Diego) has established in 1999 a non-profit organization – **the California Innocence Project (CIP)** to deal with *wrongful convictions.*

- Each year, CIP reviews more than 2000 claims of innocence from inmates convicted in Southern California.

- Moreover, CIP lobbies for law reforms that aim to prevent wrongful convictions, freeing the innocent, and helping exonerees.

Criminal justice reform

- Over many years, California lawmakers and voters adopted a series of laws that prioritized punishment over rehabilitation. This process led to overcrowding in state prisons and also disproportionately impacted **Black and Latin communities**.

- Major reforms to California's criminal justice system take effect *from January 1, 2021.*

- They refer to clearing criminal records and restoring rights, law enforcement practices, sentencing, and youth offenders. These reforms intend to shift the criminal justice system's focus *from punishment and systematic bias to rehabilitation, reducing recidivism and equal treatment regardless of race or income.*

CHAPTER 9

CALIFORNIA LEGISLATIVE BRANCH

Introduction

- The **Legislature** is a body of members with the power to make laws for political entities such as the country's state.

- Legislature forms an essential part of the government. In the separation of power model, which Montesquieu gave, they are often compared with the executive branch and the judicial branch of parliamentary government.

- The Legislature has *four core functions* to perform well for a political entity, country, or state.

- These functions are: electoral representation of the particular area, authorization of budget for country or state, **policymaking** to run that political entity, and last but not least to oversight of the assessment, monitoring, and implementation process relating to the laws and government policies.

Policymaking process

- All **legislations** begin with an idea or thought. These ideas or thoughts may come from a variety of sources.

- The process began with any legislation when Senator or Assembly member decided to author a **bill**. A legislature sends his/her idea to Legislature Council, where this idea is drafted into a bill.

- Then returned to the Legislature for introduction in assembly. If the bill's author is Senator, then the bill will initiate in Senate, and if the author is a member of the Lower House, then the bill is presented to the lower house as well.

- Any **bill** requires an expenditure of state fund must also be introduced for hearing in house's fiscal Committee, Senate Appropriate or Assembly Appropriate. Both houses have their own policy committee and fiscal Committee.

- When the Committee hears the bill, the bill author gives an argument in favor of the bill, and the Committee hears the *opposite views* about the bill.

- The Committee then **votes** by passing the bill.

- The Committee can **amend** the bill or **reject** the bill by votes.

Approving a bill

- For making law in any state or country, the final approval is required from the constitutional head of the state or country.

- In the California State Assembly case, the bill is sent to the Governor of California for final approval.

- The Governor of California has three choices.

- The Governor can sign the bill to become law, allow it to become law without his/her signature, or veto it.

- The Governor's veto can be overthrown by the vote of a two-thirds majority in the house. In California, the bill normally goes into effect on January 1, but in some urgent cases, the bill becomes law after the consent of the Governor.

Annual budget

- The **fiscal year** of California starts on July 1 and ends on June 30. A budget is a financial plan of expenditure and income in a given set of periods, usually a year.

- If a state is giving a **budget**, then it will propose all its expenditure that where its money will be spent throughout a year.

- The budget also includes a state's income than how the state will generate its money to spend a year.

- After *approving a budget*, then a state's fiscal year started.

- The final process to implement the budget is **the Governor's signature on the budget.**

- The Governor has 12 working days to sign on the budget bill or using his/her authority to "*blue pencil*" (reduce or eliminate) any appropriate constrain in the budget.

- The Legislature has authority to **override veto any blue pencil item** of Governor by giving 2/3 vote.

California Constituency influence the Legislature

- In California, the role of **constituency** in legislation is observed. People from different constituencies give their opinion about legislation, and even they influence their legislators to act like what they want in assembly. *The process to influence may differ in different constituencies*, but their role has been little increased in modern times to influence the legislators.

- People influence legislator through local meetings during election campaigning and let their legislator know what their community or constituency want and give their opinion.

- People follow the law-making process through media and **get involved** in giving their opinion on any law or legislation.

Leadership and structure of the Legislature

- The **State Legislature** in California consists of two houses, the lower house, California State Assembly, 80 members; and the upper house, California State Senate, with 40 members.

- The meeting point of both houses is in Sacramento, the Capital of California state.

- The **Speaker** is the most crucial person in the State Assembly in California. The assembly members usually elect him or her at the start of the two-year legislative term. He or she *presides over floor sessions* and constitute committees in the assembly.

- The Speaker is followed by Speaker pro Tempore, appointed by the speaker himself/herself, and presided the session in the absence of the speaker.

- California is divided into *53 congressional districts*. Each district elects a representative to serve in the United States House of Representatives as part of California's congressional Delegation.

- California's current districts were drawn in 2011 by a **California Citizens Redistricting Commission**.

- The **majority party caucus** elects the majority Floor leader. It also represents the speaker on the floor, starts the assembly procession through parliamentary procedures.

- The **minority floor leader** is elected by minority party caucus.

- Some other important people in an assembly are the Majority Whip, Minority Whip, Assistant Majority Whip, Assistant Minority Whip, and more.

Fundamental concepts

1. Bipartisanship.
2. Gerrymandering.
3. Caucus.
4. Statute.
5. Party caucus.
6. Trifecta.
7. Supermajority.
8. Redistricting.
9. Stakeholder.
10. Fiscal year.
11. Incumbents.

CHAPTER 10

THE CALIFORNIA BUDGET PROCESS

Introduction

- The **state budget** is probably the most crucial piece of legislation that the California state can enact.

- Passing the budget is essential to run the projects that keep things working as expected.

- It expresses on the spending side a set of priorities for the use of public resources.

- At the same time, it provides a variety of incentives and disincentives for various activities on the tax side.

Basics of drafting a budget

- Passing the budget implies various challenging decisions and trade-offs and includes economic assumptions, revenues, and expenditures.

- The budget in California is formed in 4 fundamental steps:

  1. The Governor formulates his state budget with the support of the Department of Finance.

  2. He then sends the budget to the Legislature each January. Each May, he publishes the May revision, which contains any changes made to the original version.

3. Third, the governor signs or vetoes the budget. If he signs the budget, he still can use his line-item veto to lower any line item.

4. Finally, the agencies implement the budget as passed, including any control language with directions for studies that have to be presented to the Legislature.

- If the balance goes negative in the **General Fund**, the state must obtain added funds by borrowing money to cover its ongoing and future projects.

- Through external borrowing, it can do so by obtaining the funds from "Wall Street" or through internal borrowing from other funds that California operates outside the General Fund.

- The California state already *has many earmarked funds set up by the Legislature for particular purposes.*

- These funds may have specific tax or fee sources, and they will likely have positive cash balances in them at any moment in time.

- In the **case of cash deficiency** in the General Fund, the state controller can temporarily borrow from these other funds to cover the deficiency adequately.

- The **California state legislature** is also different from the United States Congress.

- It is term-limited, and the Governor has a line-item veto, which allows him to cut or eliminate any item in a budget bill without rejecting the whole bill.

- It is worth considering that both houses are based on population, and California also has the **initiative process** that allows the legislative process to be bypassed, most often by interests with deep pockets.

Legislative process

- The government process by which bills are considered and laws are enacted is known as the **Legislative Process**, which starts when an Assembly Member or Senator decides to write a bill and later passes the idea for the bill to the Legislative Counsel where it is drafted into the actual bill.

- The **draft of the bill** is then returned to the Legislator for the introduction process. If the author is a Senator, then the bill is introduced in the Senate. If he is an Assembly Member, it is introduced in the Assembly.

- A bill is read or introduced the first time when the bill number, the author's name, and the descriptive bill title are read on the house floor. The bill is later sent to the *Office of State Printing*.

Revenue

- Today, revenue for the General Fund more or less comes primarily from three taxes: **the personal income tax** (70%), **the sales tax** (19%), and **the bank and corporation tax** (9%). These percentages may slightly differ over the years, but *proportions mostly stay the same.*

- Through a careful combination of *discretionary allocation and formula*, some **General Fund** revenue is taken off the top and diverted to another fund, known as the **Budget Stabilization Account**.

- The largest single source of revenue is the **personal income tax**, which provides almost half the general fund (which can be thought of as a checking account used for ongoing services, and California education is its most prominent Component).

- Personal income tax is *highly progressive* in California.

Expenditures, Deficits, and Debt

- Within the first ten days of the calendar year, the governor must submit to the Legislature a **unified budget** that is carefully balanced, contains a reasonable explanation for each proposed expenditure, and is accompanied by a budget bill itemizing each recommended expenditure.

- Politically speaking, one can consider *the budget a statement of priorities.* State budgets tend to express the fiscal priorities of some groups over others.

- **Education** is the most significant single expenditure in California; expenditures for K-14 education are required by Proposition 98 to be 40 percent or more of the general fund. If one includes higher education, education constitutes approximately half the state budget. Health and human services is the next largest category, followed by the courts and corrections.

- Over time, California has experienced several budget crises. By February 2004, for example, the state's budget deficit had grown massive and out of control.

- California today carries the **largest state debt burden in the country** and is also among only a few states that have borrowed close to a budget gap.

- It is worth considering that the California state has long featured sloppy budgetary language when it comes to **deficits and surpluses**.

Political problems with Budgeting

- Three major kinds of problems confront California's various local governments.

- **First**, the *extreme polarization in regional political cultures* across the state makes legislative compromise and consensus building difficult, as illustrated by the stark differences in partisanship, political tolerance, and voting tendencies observed in San Francisco, Los Angeles County, and San Diego County.

- The **second** is the challenge posed by *internal conflicts and secessionist movements in some local jurisdictions*, as illustrated by the recent attempt of the San Fernando Valley to secede from Los Angeles.

- The **third** is the crisis in local government finance and the threat to effective home rule caused by the *worsening state budget deficit* and the state government's efforts to solve it by seizing property tax revenues from county and city governments.

- Given the current blue state politics in California, the **Democrats** greatly influence the state policymaking process.

- In its present-day political configuration, the California Legislature is mostly dominated by Democrats. The Democratic leadership and the California governor will confer on what is acceptable to the latter.

- One should consider that *only a simple majority in the Legislature* is needed to pass a budget.

- There are five relevant players in the budget game in California: *the governor and the four leaders of both parties in both houses of the Legislature.*

- The need for one or *two marginal votes* may create even more fundamental players.

- Because of his role at both ends of the budgetary process, considering that one person is required to broker the deal, the Governor is usually the key player. However, even he can be held hostage by other recalcitrant legislators.

Taxation in California

- Even though it is a fact that Californians pay high taxes, it is a controversial topic to argue that **Californians are overtaxed**.

- The state has cut taxes several times in the last decade, not raised them, as the state received more revenues than it expected.

- The tax is low *for middle-class families that have little or no tax until they earn more than $45,000*; the tax load from the state and local governments in California is about average among the fifty states, and sometimes, even below average.

- The highest-income Californians continue to pay a considerable share of California's personal income tax.

- For the 2018 California tax year, **the top one percent of income earners paid around 46 percent** of personal income taxes.

- It is essential to consider that those California **top earners** tend to derive *significant incomes from financial markets*.

- Consequently, the ups and downs of the stock market can strongly affect **personal income tax collections**.

- As a result, budget forecasting ultimately involves projecting trends in the real economy and financial booms, cycles, and busts.

- The **overall California tax structure**, compared with other states, is more dependent on volatile taxes; they go up and down with the economy (income tax and sales tax) and less dependent on taxes that do not vary with the economy (the property tax), because of the *Proposition 13 limits*.

- While most states that rank high on the scale of taxes per $1,000 of personal income are low-income states like South Carolina, California is generally considered a rich one.

Chapter 11

GOVERNMENT IN CALIFORNIA

Structure

- California is divided into *58 counties*. According to the California Constitution, a county makes and enforces local ordinances that do not conflict with general laws.

- A county also has the power to sue and be sued, purchase and hold land, manage or dispose of its properties, and levy and collect taxes authorized by law.

County and city

- In California, there is a distinction between a **county** and a **city**. In contrast to Californian cities, counties do not have broad powers of self-government.

- There is also more strict legislative control over counties. The **Legislature** can delegate or take back to the counties any of the functions which *belong to the state itself*.

Types of Counties in California

- The California Constitution recognizes **two types of counties**: general law counties and charter counties.

- There are currently *44 general law counties and 14 charter counties*.

- **General law counties** are under the jurisdiction of state law as to the number and duties of county elected officials.

- **Charter counties** have a limited degree of "home rule" authority that may provide for the election, compensation, terms, removal, and salary of the governing Board; for the election or appointment (except the sheriff, district attorney, and assessor who must be elected), compensation, terms and removal of all county officers.

Counties in California

- A **county** may adopt, amend or repeal a charter with majority vote approval. When counties do not have a charter or, in the case of potential amendment or repeal, such initiative can be proposed by the **Board of Supervisors** or a **charter commission**.

- The **amendment** or **repeal of a charter** can also be proposed through an initiative petition. The initiative petition can be used if citizens of a county want to determine whether to draft or revise a charter and elect a charter commission on the ballot.

- If this question receives majority support, the 15 candidates for the charter commission who receive the most votes will organize into a commission to prepare a charter.

The Board of Supervisors

- The **Board of Supervisors** represents *both the legislative and the executive authority* of the county.

- It has quasi-judicial authority.

- A Board of Supervisors needs to consist of **five members**.

- This general law is provided to all law and charter counties, except the charter provides otherwise.

- To be a **board member**, one needs to be a registered voter of, and reside in, the district from which the member is elected.

- If a county charter does not define a method of filling vacancies, the *Governor appoints a successor*.

- The Board of Supervisors can only perform during their meetings. Individual members of the Board do not have the power to act for the county.

- Meetings are open and public. They are *recorded and archived*

- In terms of the county's legislative body, the Board of Supervisors may act by **resolution, board order, or ordinance.**

- A **resolution** is a declaration about future purposes or proceedings of the Board or a policy statement by the Board.

- Resolutions are often used when the Board makes specific findings of *Supervisors*. A **board order** is usually a directive from the Board of Supervisors to its subordinate county officers.

Municipalities in California

- California consists of **482 municipalities.**

- California law makes no distinction between *"city"* and *"town"*, and municipalities may use either term in their official names.

- As in counties, cities derive their power from either the California Government Code (statute) or from adopting a city charter.

- One can distinguish different forms of cities in California: *general law cities, charter cities, and consolidated city and county.*

Fundamental concepts

- Contract cities.

- Independent cities.

- Unincorporated areas.

Municipal government

- In a **council-manager form of government**, the council is the governing body of the city, elected by the public. the city manager is not an elected position.

- Instead, the holder of this office serves at the pleasure of the council, which retains the legal right to dismiss and replace the city manager. The hiring process for a city manager begins with **general discussions among city council members,** *often in consultation with voters and professional consultants.*

- After a hiring notice is drafted and distributed to professional organizations, the process then moves to a **multistage interview** process that includes *a review of applications and onsite interviews with qualified candidates.*

- The process ends with a **vote taken** by the city council.

- The **council** is responsible for providing legislative direction to the city.

- The mayor and council, as a *collegian body*, are responsible for setting policy, approving the budget, and determining the tax rate.

- The role of the **manager** is administrative operations of the city based on the council's recommendations.

- The manager serves as the *council's chief advisor.* Managers are responsible for preparing the budget, directing day-to-day operations, and hiring and firing personnel.

- The **mayor-council form of government** is the form that most closely reflects the American federal government with an elected legislature and a separately elected Executive.

- Mayor-council governments are more prominent in older and larger cities, as well as cities located in the Mid-Atlantic and Midwest.

- Among major cities in California, this model is present in *Los Angeles, San Diego, San Francisco.*

- The **mayor or elected executive** is the head of the city or *county government.*

- The extent of his or her authority can vary from purely representative functions to full responsibility for most operations.

- The executive body or mayor is usually **responsible** for: hiring and firing department heads, preparation and administration of the budget, and veto power (which may be overridden) over acts of the legislature.

Special districts

- Special districts refer to public agencies that provide one or more specific services to a community, such as water service, sewer service, parks, fire protection, and others.

- California has almost **3300 special districts**.

- There are mainly three types of special districts: *dependent, independent, and enterprise special districts.*

- Most special districts perform a single function, such as water service, parks, and recreation, fire protection, pest abatement, or cemetery management. Others have multiple functions.

Federalism in California Government

- **Regional** and **local** governments work together in California at multiple levels to solve the problems of the citizens.

- The regional governmental organizations are utilized by local governments to make regional improvements including in *transportation, air quality, and economic development*, among others.

- A **mandate** is a requirement by the state government directing the local government to provide a service or a higher level of an existing service.

- The **state** imposes a mandate directly on local agencies; in other words, such mandates are not the result of a new federal law or a voter approved state initiative but rather *new state legislation or state regulations*.

Tribal governments

- California has the highest Native American population in the country and **every tribe has its own government**.

- According to the 2010 U.S. Census, *California represents 12 percent of the total Native American population (approximately 720,000)* identified themselves as Native American.

- Over one-half of the state's Native American population is composed of individuals (and now their descendants) who were relocated to large urban areas as part of the federal government's termination policy.

- There are **109 federally recognized Indian tribes in California** and several non-federally recognized tribes petitioning for federal recognition through the Bureau of Indian Affairs-Office of Federal Recognition.

- Tribes in California currently have nearly **100 separate reservations or rancherias**.

- There are also a number of individual Indian trust allotments.

MC QUESTIONS

Chapter 1

1. Which expedition proved that California was a peninsula?

    a. The expedition of Juan Rodríguez Cabrillo

    b. The expedition of Hernan Cortes

    c. The expedition of Francisco de Ulloa

    d. None of the above

2. Cortes described the Californian land as:

    a. hot, dry, and sterile

    b. hot, humid, and sterile

    c. cold, dry, and sterile

    d. cold, humid, and sterile

3. True or False: The period before the Spanish expeditions touched the land of California, and Native Americans are known as the Kumeyaay people, which populated this area.

4. True or False: The death of Padre Sarria is considered one of the most important events in the period of decline of the Missions.

5. True or False: Years before the arrival of the first Europeans on Californian land, the South Bay was inhabited by a large African population.

6. True or False. At the beginning of the 20th century, the Spanish colonies in America struggled for their independence.

7. True or False: The Mission of San Fernandoincluded people from some rancherias or villages, including Cahuenga, Topanga, and Camulos.

8. True or False: The Mission of San Fernando Rey de Espana was founded on September 8, 1697, by the Franciscans.

9. The last governor sent to California from Mexico was _____

    a. Francisco Carvajal

    b. John Gilroy

    c. Manuel Micheltorena

    d. Arturo Michelena

10. Mexico lost about _____ of its territory due to the Mexican-American War.

    a. one-third

    b. two-thirds

    c. one-fifth

    d. half

11. Texas gained its independence from Mexico in ____.

    a. 1712

    b. 1836

    c. 1854

    d. None of the above

12. The Treaty of Guadalupe Hidalgo was signed on _____.

    a. December 15, 1899

    b. June 25, 1812

    c. February 2, 1848

    d. March 15, 1832

13. In 1848, Mexico made significant concessions in favor of America, giving Mexico, Utah, Nevada, Arizona, California, Texas, and Western Colorado for _____.

   a. $50 million

   b. $5 million.

   c. $15 million.

   d. None of the above.

14. True or False: Like the mission system, Africans and Chinese provided the biggest part of the working force for the emerging ranching economy.

15. True or False: The symbol of the new emerging culture was the Californian ranchero.

16. True or False: The year 1821 is known as the year when Mexico achieved independence, and this news reached Alta California in the following year.

Chapter 2

1. By 1877 the Southern Pacific possessed _____ of California's railroad mileage.

   a. 85%

   b. 50%

   c. 15%

   d. None of the above

2. True or False: The construction of the Southern Pacific Railroad can be considered a realization of the Manifest Destiny.

3. True or False: The Southern Pacific helped California to move from a once-isolated place to a significant economic and political force and helped lead to the state's rapid growth.

4. _____, a civil engineer who designed California's first railroad, promoted Route 41, passing through Nebraska, Wyoming, Utah, Nevada, and California.

   a. Charles Crocker

   b. Theodore Judah

    c. Leland Stanford

    d. None of the above

5. True or False: The build of the Central Pacific helped to develop a policy of capital investments with foreign funds.

6. True or False: Before the construction of the transcontinental railway, diseases were uncommon in California.

7. The Union Pacific from Omaha and the Central Pacific East from Sacramento received government bonds of _____ for a mile-built route.

    a. $160,000

    b. $50,000

    c. $32,000

    d. $16,000

8. The Central Pacific was led by the so-called "Big Four": Who were the Big Four?

    a. Collis P. Huntington, Mark Hopkins, Leland Stanford, and Charles Crocker.

    b. Collis P. Huntington, Donald Trump, Leland Stanford, and Charles Crocker.

    c. Theodore Judah, Mark Hopkins, Leland Stanford, and Charles Crocker.

    d. Collis P. Huntington, Daniel Strong, Leland Stanford, and Charles Crocker.

9. Huntington from New York was responsible for _____.

    a. Took care of the accounts.

    b. Raising capital.

    c. Construction works.

    d. None of the above.

10. Judah did not survive the business trip to New York City due to _____.

    a. yellow fever.

    b. tuberculosis.

    c. a car crash.

    d. an assault.

11. The Central Pacific Railway started operating on _____.

    a. October 12, 1844

    b. June 3, 1853

    c. October 6, 1863

    d. October 26, 1863

12. The Treaty of Guadalupe Hidalgo was signed on _____.

    a. December 15, 1899

    b. June 25, 1812

    c. February 2, 1848

    d. March 15, 1832

13. True or False: The Southern Pacific was acquired by the Union Pacific Corporation in 1996

14. True or False: By early 1899, the Central Pacific and Union Pacific were closing in on each other across northern Utah, aided by a Mormon workforce under contract to both companies.

15. True or False: The construction of the railway in the Central Pacific has faced different types of problems and obstacles in terms of penetration through mountains, gorges, snow cover, etcetera.

Chapter 3

1. After the year _____, Californians envied the 63 progressive movements already taking place in other states.

    a. 1900.

    b. 1910.

    c. 1899.

    d. 1890.

2. True or False: Californians were particularly impressed by how the state of Wisconsin under Governor Robert La Follett was led.

3. True or False: During the XIX century, corruption in California was not widespread.

4. True or False: For most Californians, the railroad was at that time a simple technology whose sole purpose was to transport people.

5. True or False: The railroad was the largest employer in California.

6. Hiram Johnson was the leader of the _____ party in California.

    a. Republican.

    b. Democratic.

    c. Progressive.

    d. None of the above.

7. Johnson's election as Governor of California in ___ marked a turning point in California's overall political history.

    a. 1910.

    b. 1915.

    c. 1900.

    d. 1920.

8. True or False: Johnson has been known for his interventionist political stances.

9. True or False: Johnson opposed U.S. support for the Treaty of Versailles, the League of Nations, and the World Court.

10. True or False: Johnson's progressive reforms were an important step towards a revision of the state's Constitution in 1911.

11. The method and level of support for state and local governments were changed radically in 1978 by _____.

    a. Proposition 13.

    b. Proposition 10.

    c. Proposition 15.

    d. None of the above.

12. Around _____ of Californians considered that Proposition 13's supermajority requirement for new special taxes had had a good effect on local government services provided to residents.

    a. 60%

    b. 50%.

    c. 70%.

    d. 25%.

13. Proposition 13 is quite _____ in California.

    a. rejected.

    b. misunderstood.

    c. polarizing.

    d. popular.

14. True or False: The widespread corruption in government associated with the political patronage, the sowing immigration rate, and the rise of the middle class contributed to declining the patronage system.

15. True or False: The most significant part of the XIX century, federal workers were a marginal political weapon.

16. True or False: Since the first days of the Republic, the patronage system was considered an imminent method for filling federal positions.

Chapter 4

1. Illegal border crossings increased from _____ in the 1970s to _____ in 1999.

    a. 200,000, 1.5 million.

    b. 500,000, 1.5 million.

    c. 200,000, 2 million.

    d. 500,000, 1 million.

2. In 1997, the number of illegal migrants in the United States was estimated at
   _____.

   a. 5 million.

   b. 2 million.

   c. 2.5 million.

   d. 3.1 million.

3. True or False: The foreign-born population in 1960 was composed mainly of the elderly survivors of the early 20th-century immigration.

4. True or False: Gentrification is a process of changes in the neighborhood that implicates economic changes in what used to be a historically not so developed area, in terms of real estate investment and new higher-income residents moving in.

5. Conservatives estimate that migration will add over _____ immigrants to rural areas by 2020.

   a. 2 million

   b. 5 million

   c. 10 million

   d. None of the above.

6. True or False: Latino immigrants in the United States are concentrated in smaller cities.

7. True or False: Newcomers often have different views on many issues from the natives, such as environment, community understanding, economic development.

8. True or False: Until the 1990s, the reasons for the return to rural areas were related to geopolitical events.

9. Of all the new positions in California in the 1970s, nearly _____ were held by Mexican immigrants.

   a. half

   b. one-fifth

   c. one-third

   d. one-fourth

10. The 1970s were marked by lightning-fast job expansion in Southern California_____ of these jobs were the so-called white-collar jobs.

    a. Two-thirds

    b. Half

    c. One-third

    d. None of the above

11. The 1980 census shows that immigrants from Mexico spoke very little English. _____ did not speak English at all.

    a. one-third

    b. two-thirds

    c. one-fifth

    d. None of the above

12. True or False: By 1994, prices for migrant smuggling were around $1000.

13. True or False: Western Mexico, and especially the states of Michoacán, Jalisco, and Guanajuato, is a source of immigrants to the United States.

14. True or False: Gentrification processes are pretty complex, and there is a lack of professional literature for their understanding.

15. True or False: The 2000s were marked by lightning-fast job expansion in Southern Californi

16. True or False: Of U.S.-born whites, only one-fifth worked in positions classified as unskilled.

Chapter 5

1. According to _____ from the Californian Constitution, the citizens of this country have the right to initiate a recall election.

    a. Article 10.

    b. Article 5.

    c. Article 7.

    d. Article 2.

2. In Los Angeles, the threshold for a recall is ___ of signatures

   a. 25%.

   b. 50%.

   c. 10%.

   d. None of the above.

3. True or False: In California, the Supreme court has used the First Amendment right of association and ruled that political parties in California have a constitutional right to exclude non-party members in primary elections.

4. True or False: Direct primary elections were introduced in 1901 as a reform of the progressive era.

5. True or False: Under new California laws, voters receive by mail sample primary ballots.

6. Since 1913, there have been _____ recall attempts of state elected officials in California.

   a. 100.

   b. 150.

   c. 179.

   d. None of the above.

7. The procedure to recall a state official is the following: first, the proponent fills a notice of intent to recall a petition that needs to be signed by ___ voters to start the petition drive process.

   a. 150.

   b. 100.

   c. 50.

   d. 65.

8. True or False: The impeachments in principle form a bipolar image of corrupt politicians and a united, morally superior citizenship.

9. True or False: The model of procedural democracy does not favor democratic procedures over the quality of the decisions they produce.

10. True or False: The recalls are a product of the dramatic fusion between representative institutions and direct democracy.

11. True or False: A recall is a radical act, and provides a new form of analysis of the important issues for the design of democratic institutions.

12. In _____, California became the first state to guarantee equal suffrage for women and men.

    a. 1911.

    b. 1900.

    c. 1890.

    d. 1954.

13. Cross-filling was introduced in California in _____.

    a. 1900.

    b. 1913.

    c. 1905.

    d. None of the above.

14. True or False: Proposition 62 referred to a single primary ballot in which all state and congressional candidates are presented together, no matter their party affiliation.

15. True or False: The very act of recall represents an increase in lawsuits as a political weapon.

16. True or False: The constitution of the United States itself allows a recall of any federally elected official.

Chapter 6

1. When proponents collect _____ of the signatures required, they have to notify the Secretary of State.

    a. 25%

    b. 50%

    c. 40%

    d. 75%

2. True or False: An initiative that has been certified by county officials to have been signed by the requisite number of voters is classified by the Secretary of State as 'eligible' for the following state-wide ballot.

3. True or False: Direct initiatives are an irrelevant feature in California's public policy.

4. True or False: Citizens in California can remove their state and local officials before their term expires.

5. True or False: Scholars supporting direct democracy argue that initiatives can offer citizens the chance to override the decisions of elected officials so that representatives will be more aware of the different views in society.

6. Verification of the signatures occurs via a random sample of ___ signatures or at least ___ of the total amount collected (whichever is great) within ___ days.

   a. 500, 3%, 30.

   b. 5000, 5%, 90.

   c. 1000, 3%, 30.

   d. None of the above.

7. If valid signatures are less than _____, the initiative fails.

   a. 70%

   b. 95%.

   c. 90%.

   d. 80%.

8. Acknowledging the _____ nature of California's democracy does not entail that direct initiatives are just tools in the hands of a few political elites.

   a. complex.

   b. rich.

   c. diverse.

   d. hybrid.

9. True or False: The populist paradox suggests that special interests can buy influence through the initiative process by affecting information available to make political decisions.

10. True or False: Since its adoption, there have been no proposals concerning how to improve each phase of the initiative process in California.

11. True or False: The most expensive Proposition in California history was Proposition 30 in 2012.

12. True or False: Once the Governor receives all documents, a notice for the recall election is published not less than 60 days nor more than 80 days from the date of certification of sufficient signatures.

13. In California, the election must take place within _____ days from the date of certification.

    a. 180.

    b. 200.

    c. 60.

    d. 90.

14. Proposition 15 raised approximately _____ in support.

    a. 130 million.

    b. 10 million.

    c. 50 million.

    d. 69 million.

15. True or False: Since the first one in 1912, only 89 optional referendums have been proposed, of which 50 qualified for the ballot.

Chapter 7

1. California's current Constitution was adopted in _____.

    a. 1810.

    b. 1912.

    c. 1850.

    d. 1879.

2. California's Constitution has been revised ____ times as of 2020

   a. 200

   b. 300

   c. 516

   d. 450

3. The California executive branch is made up of over _____ state institutions.

   a. 200

   b. 100

   c. 50

   d. None of the above.

4. True or False: The Governor of California is elected by the people of California and is limited to two five-year terms.

5. True or False: More than any other state, California has contributed more citizens to the American national defense since joining the Union.

6. True or False: The Governor is the State's Commander-in-Chief.

7. True or False: In the event of a vacancy, the Lieutenant Governor cannot become Governor.

8. California's insurance sector is worth _____ each year and contributes considerably to the State's economy.

   a. $123 billion

   b. $223 billion

   c. $250 billion

   d. $137 billion

9. The California State Legislature was founded in _____.

   a. 1910.

   b. 430.

   c. 1810.

   d. 1849.

10. True or False: The people of California elect the branch's executive authorities, such as the Governor, Lieutenant Governor, Secretary of State, and Attorney General.

11. True or False: Governors are elected by popular vote for a four-year term, with a two-term limit if elected after June 6, 1950.

12. True or False: The Governor's authority over executive branch duties in the State is subject to legislative review.

13. The _____ is California's chief elections officer.

    a. Governor.

    b. Secretary of State.

    c. Lieutenant.

    d. None of the above.

14. The Insurance Commissioner licenses more than _____ agents, brokers, solicitors, and bail bond agents in the State and insurance and title firms to do business in California.

    a. 200,000.

    b. 100,000.

    c. 400,000.

    d. 1,000,000.

15. The California Department of Forestry and Fire Protection is in charge of fire prevention in a total of _____ under state control and the management of the State's private and public forests.

    a. 10 million acres.

    b. 45 million acres.

    c. 31 million acres.

    d. None of the above.

16. True or False: The Treasurer heads and supervises authorities that fund various programs, including education, health care, affordable housing, transportation, economic development, alternative energy, and pollution cleanup.

17. True or False: The Treasure carefully supervises, controls and heads private enterprises in California.

Chapter 8

1. Based on the official statistics of the judiciary in California, the Supreme Court deals with approximately _____ cases per year.

    a. 9000.

    b. 3000.

    c. 2000.

    d. 5000.

2. A justice also comes before the voters at the end of his or her _____ term.

    a. 12-year.

    b. 6-year.

    c. 3-year.

    d. None of the above.

3. True or False: The Supreme Court is the state's highest court.

4. True or False: Collaborative courts (also known as problem-solving courts) combine judicial supervision with rehabilitation services.

5. True or False: In neutral evaluation, only one party gets a chance to present the case to an unbiased person.

6. In each Court of Appeal, a panel of ___ judges (justices) decides appeals from trial courts.

    a. 5.

    b. 10.

    c. 6.

    d. 3.

7. In the whole state of California, there are ____ superior courts, 1 in each county.

    a. 58.

    b. 60.

    c. 45.

    d. 20.

8. True or False: Trial court judges are elected at a general election by voters of the county on a nonpartisan ballot.

9. True or False: Trial courts are not superior courts.

10. True or False: The state court system in California has four types of different courts.

11. True or False: When a defendant loses a case or part of a case in the trial court, one can appeal this decision in a higher court (an appellate court) to review the trial court's decision.

12. If the defendant is not in custody at the arraignment, the trial must start within ____ days of arraignment or plea, whichever is later.

    a. 45.

    b. 10.

    c. 15.

    d. 30.

13. The trial must start within ____ days of the arraignment on the Information.

    a. 120

    b. 60.

    c. 90.

    d. 30.

14. In California, the Grand Jury system consists of ____ grand separate juries.

    a. 20.

    b. 30.

    c. 58.

    d. 70.

15. True or False: There are 100 state prisons in California.

16. True or False: Prison camps are mostly connected to the state prison system, and they house low-security level inmates.

17. True or False: Each year, CIP reviews more than 2000 claims of innocence from inmates convicted in Southern California.

Chapter 9

1. The First California Legislature planned to meet in _____ in 1849.

    a. San Bernardino.

    b. San Jose.

    c. Los Angeles.

    d. None of the above.

2. The fiscal year of California starts on _____ and ends on _____.

    a. June 30, April 5.

    b. July 30, June 1.

    c. June 1, June 30.

    d. July 1, June 30.

3. A _____ is a financial plan of expenditure and income in a given set of periods.

    a. budget.

    b. proposal.

    c. resolution.

    d. None of the above.

4. True or False: California is the third largest state in the United States of America population-wise.

5. True or False: California is the 5th largest economy globally (state-wise)

6. True or False: Before introducing a bill in Committee, there is an analysis of existing laws about those matters, required laws, and some background information about the bill.

7. True or False: The annual state budget, next to the state constitution, is the most crucial document in Californi

8. Any law passed by a legislature of a country is known as a statute.

    a. resolution.

    b. proposal.

    c. statute.

    d. bill.

9. True or False: Gerrymandering is a political process in which one faction of society gets benefits from the particular laws enacted in the Legislature.

10. The California budget size is _____ dollars which is more than most of the countries in the world.

    a. 54.3 billion.

    b. 85 billion.

    c. 100 billion

    d. 34.5 billion.

11. The Legislative must submit its budget to the Governor of California on _____.

    a. January 5.

    b. January 10.

    c. January 15.

    d. January 30.

12. Governor has ___ working days to sign the budget bill.

    a. 12.

    b. 15.

    c. 3.

    d. 5.

13. True or False: The Speaker is the most crucial person in the State Assembly in California.

14. True or False: Caucus is taken from the French language, which means a gathering of tribal leaders to discuss any matters.

15. True or False: A supermajority or qualified majority is a specified majority to gain voters' support more than fifty percent.

16. True or False: The process of making an idea of any law into law is called law-making.

Chapter 10

1. Each _____, the California Governor publishes the May revision, which contains any changes made to the state budget since its publication in January.

    a. November

    b. February

    c. June

    d. May

2. In California, there are ___ Senators and ___ Assembly Members representing the people

    a. 40, 80.

    b. 20, 100.

    c. 30, 70.

    d. 50, 120.

3. True or False: California is considered a low-income state.

4. True or False: The overall California tax structure, compared with other states, is more dependent on volatile taxes.

5. True or False: It is very common that the Assembly and Senate drafts of the budget differ.

6. Bills that immediately take effect or require an appropriation usually require ___ votes in the Senate and ___ votes in the Assembly to be passed.

    a. 50, 100.

b. 60, 120.

c. 34, 56.

d. 27, 54.

7. Generally, expenditures from the General Fund account for about ___% of all state expenditures.

    a. 69

    b. 40

    c. 80

    d. 90

8. True or False: Not even during a budget crisis, the fiscal year can end with a deficiency.

9. True or False: If the balance goes negative in the General Fund, the state must obtain added funds by borrowing money to cover its ongoing and future projects.

10. True or False: In California, as in most states in the United States of America, the Governor has a line item veto in appropriations, including those in the state budget.

11. Since the passage of _____, the state government has considerably received less revenue, which has since then become more volatile, rising and falling with the state economy.

    a. Proposition 5.

    b. Proposition 9.

    c. Proposition 10.

    d. Proposition 13.

12. Today, revenue for the General Fund comes primarily from the _____.

    a. sales tax.

    b. personal income tax.

    c. bank and corporation tax.

    d. None of the above.

13. Within the first _____ days of the calendar year, the governor must submit to the Legislature a unified budget.

    a. ten.

    b. thirty.

    c. five.

    d. three,

14. True or False: The total amount of federal stimulus funds for California state programs is today close to $275 billion.

15. True or False: Personal income tax is not highly progressive in California.

16. True or False: The state budget is prepared and sent to the California Legislature by January 15, with revisions later in the spring as the financial outlook becomes clearer.

17. California has a labor force of ___ million.

    a. 30.

    b. 15.

    c. 25.

    d. 19.5.

18. California now has a projected _____ surplus.

    a. $75.7 billion.

    b. $100 billion.

    c. $55 billion.

    d. $92.5 billion.

19. True or False: In its present-day political configuration, the California Legislature is mostly dominated by Democrats.

20. The governor appoints members to approximately _____ boards and commissions.

    a. 100

    b. 225

    c. 300

    d. 325

Chapter 11

1. The most populous county in California is _____.

   a. Los Angeles County

   b. San Diego County

   c. Riverside County

   d. Orange County

2. True or False: California represents 12 percent of the United States' total Native American population.

3. Tribes in California currently have nearly _____ separate reservations or rancherias.

   a. 1000

   b. 20

   c. 50

   d. 100

4. True or False: According to the California Constitution, a county makes and enforces local ordinances that do not conflict with general laws.

5. True or False: The Board of Supervisors only represents the legislative authority of the county.

6. California is divided into _____ counties.

   a. 58

   b. 72

   c. 13

   d. 45

7. A _____ is a declaration about future purposes or proceedings of the Board or a policy statement by the Board.

   a. order

   b. resolution

   c. sentence

   d. None of the above

8. California consists of _____ municipalities.

   a. 132

   b. 213

   c. 100

   d. 482

9. True or False: A contract city is a city that contracts for the provision of one or more municipal services with another unit of government or with a private or commercial organization.

10. True or False: The mayor and council, as a collegial body, are responsible for setting policy, approving the budget, and determining the tax rate.

11. California has almost ____ special districts.

   a. 1300.

   b. 1000.

   c. 3300.

   d. 4000.

12. The concept of joint power authorities was created in 1921 after _____ was passed.

   a. Bill 18.

   b. Bill 15.

   c. Bill 20.

   d. Bill 25.

13. True or False: Most special districts perform a single function, such as water service, parks, and recreation, fire protection, pest abatement, or cemetery management.

14. True or False: The mayor is considered as the political head of the municipality but his/her role is rather legislative and does not have the power to veto legislative actions.

15. True or False: Charter counties have a limited degree of "home rule" authority that may provide for the election, compensation, terms, removal, and salary of the governing Board.

ANSWERS

Chapter 1

1. C
2. A
3. T
4. T
5. F
6. F
7. T
8. F
9. C
10. A
11. B
12. C
13. C
14. F
15. T
16. T

Chapter 2

1. A
2. T
3. T
4. B
5. F
6. F
7. D
8. A
9. B
10. A
11. C
12. T
13. F
14. F
15. T

Chapter 3

1. A
2. T
3. F
4. T
5. T
6. C
7. A
8. F
9. T
10. T
11. A
12. B
13. D
14. T
15. F
16. T

Chapter 4

1. A
2. D
3. T
4. T
5. B
6. F
7. T
8. F
9. C
10. A
11. A
12. F
13. T
14. T
15. F
16. T

Chapter 5

1. D
2. A
3. T
4. F
5. T
6. C
7. D
8. T
9. F
10. T
11. F
12. A
13. B
14. T

15. T
16. F

Chapter 6

1. A
2. T
3. F
4. T
5. T
6. A
7. B
8. D
9. T
10. F
11. F
12. T
13. A
14. D
15. T

Chapter 7

1. D
2. C
3. A
4. F
5. T
6. T
7. F
8. B

9. D
10. T
11. F
12. T
13. B
14. A
15. C
16. T
17. F

Chapter 8

1. A
2. A
3. T
4. T
5. F
6. D
7. A
8. T
9. F
10. F
11. T
12. A
13. B
14. C
15. F
16. T
17. T

Chapter 9

1. B
2. D
3. A
4. F
5. T
6. T
7. T
8. C
9. T
10. A
11. B
12. A
13. T
14. F
15. T
16. T

Chapter 10

1. D
2. A
3. F
4. T
5. T
6. D
7. A
8. F
9. T

10. T
11. D
12. B
13. A
14. T
15. F
16. F
17. D
18. A
19. T
20. D

Chapter 11

1. A
2. T
3. D
4. T
5. F
6. A
7. B
8. D
9. T
10. T
11. C
12. A
13. T
14. T
15. T

ABOUT THE AUTHOR

R. L. Cohen is a university professor residing in Redlands, California. His current research focus is on political science, ethics, and religious studies. R. L. Cohen has a passion for social justice in order to create a better world for his children. When he is not lecturing, he often can be found at the beach, at a unique coffee bar, or traveling back to his home in New Zealand.

CPSIA information can be obtained
at www.ICGtesting.com
Printed in the USA
LVHW061456191022
731073LV00011B/424